FEDERAL FORCES

CAREERS AS
FEDERAL AGENTS

A CAREER AS A
BORDER PATROL AGENT

Dawn Rapine

New York

Published in 2016 by The Rosen Publishing Group, Inc.
29 East 21st Street, New York, NY 10010

First Edition

Editor: Caitlin McAneney
Book Design: Mickey Harmon

Library of Congress Cataloging-in-Publication Data

Rapine, Dawn.
 A career as a border patrol agent / Dawn Rapine.
    pages cm. — (Federal forces)
Includes bibliographical references and index.
ISBN 978-1-4994-1055-6 (pbk.)
ISBN 978-1-4994-1092-1 (6 pack)
ISBN 978-1-4994-1109-6 (library binding)
1. Border patrol agents—United States—Juvenile literature. 2. Border patrols—United States—Juvenile literature. I. Title.

JV6483.R36 2016
363.28'502373—dc23

2015009241

Manufactured in the United States of America

CPSIA Compliance Information: Batch #WS15PK: For Further Information contact Rosen Publishing, New York, New York at 1-800-237-9932

Contents

Border Country

From the arctic chill in Alaska to superhot deserts near Mexico, border country has some of the toughest landscapes and harshest conditions in the United States. Despite these conditions, people attempt to travel through these areas to enter the country without authorization. Border Patrol agents are the first line of law enforcement at the border. They watch our borders with sharp eyes and advanced technology to track people and goods that are **smuggled** across these borders.

The United States has about 7,500 miles (12,070 km) of borders, and U.S. Border Patrol—the law enforcement arm of U.S. **Customs** and Border Protection (CBP)—is responsible for security in these areas. CBP agents from other divisions **monitor** the air and oceans near U.S. borders and coastlines.

Border Patrol agents search for tunnels under the borders. Smugglers sometimes use these tunnels to transport illegal drugs, goods, or people from Mexico to the United States.

Customs and Border Protection

CBP is an agency within the Department of Homeland Security (DHS). It enforces the laws of the United States at our nation's borders and ports of entry. Millions of people and millions of tons of goods enter the United States every year, and it's the responsibility of CBP to monitor all traffic into and out of the United States. With over 60,000 employees, CBP is one of the largest agencies in DHS.

While the Border Patrol has been around since 1924, CBP wasn't established until March 1, 2003. It was a result of the Homeland Security Act that was passed after the **terrorist** attacks of September 11, 2001. It combined agents from the U.S. Border Patrol, U.S. Customs Service, and **Immigration** and Naturalization Service, as well as agricultural inspectors.

Ronald Reagan Building

CBP has its home, or headquarters, in the Ronald Reagan Building and International Trade Center. The Ronald Reagan Building is just down the road from the White House in Washington, D.C. Finished in 1998, the building was named in honor of President Ronald Reagan, who signed authorization for the building's construction in 1989. At 3.1 million square feet (287,999 sq m), it's the largest structure in Washington, D.C. It's also the official World Trade Center for Washington, D.C.

The Border Patrol can trace its history back to **Prohibition**. This picture shows customs officers in New Jersey taking illegal alcohol. Alcohol was smuggled into seaports and over the Canadian border.

The First People Visitors Meet

When international travelers visit the United States, or when Americans return, a Customs and Border Patrol officer is one of the first people they meet.

It's the responsibility of the CBP officer to determine the identity and nationality of travelers entering the United States at ports of entry and decide whether they and their belongings should be allowed into the country. The officer inspects the passports—and **visas** if necessary—of people coming into the country. They also ask questions about the person's travels out of the country and what their plans are in the United States.

The CBP officer must be very observant, since sometimes criminals such as terrorists or smugglers may try to enter the United States using

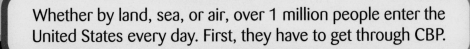

Whether by land, sea, or air, over 1 million people enter the United States every day. First, they have to get through CBP.

Along the Canadian Border

The U.S.-Canada border, also known as the International Boundary, is 5,525 miles (8,892 km) long including Alaska. That makes it the longest international border in the world. There are over 100 border-crossing stations on roads, railways, and seaports along the International Boundary. Customs and Border Patrol officers staff most of these border-crossing stations, as do officers from Canada Border Services Agency.

When alcohol was made illegal in the United States during Prohibition, bootleggers smuggled alcohol from Canada. On May 28, 1924, Congress established the U.S. Border Patrol to monitor the country's borders and inspect immigrants and goods coming from Canada.

While there are occasional unauthorized border crossings, CBP agents at the U.S.-Canada border work hard to thoroughly inspect travelers crossing the International Boundary.

The Peace Bridge is one of over 300 ports of entry in the United States. Dedicated in 1927 to celebrate 100 years of peace between the United States and Canada, the bridge crosses the Niagara River and connects Buffalo, New York, to Fort Erie, Ontario. Over 5.6 million cars, buses, and trucks crossed the Peace Bridge in 2014.

Along the Mexican Border

At the U.S.-Mexico border, it's a bit less peaceful. Many people try to cross from Mexico into the United States without authorization, sometimes to find work and other times to smuggle drugs or people into the country. Conditions can be harsh at the U.S.-Mexico border, which is 1,989 miles (3,200 km) long. The temperatures can be over 100 degrees Fahrenheit (38 degrees Celsius) during the day, but below freezing at night.

Border Patrol agents stop and sometimes inspect **vehicles** coming from the border. Agents also go into the wilderness to track and catch people crossing the border on foot. Often they find people who are sick or injured and need assistance before they're inspected. Agents must balance the need to help ill but illegal visitors with their job of securing the border.

Border Patrol agents use many kinds of transportation while surveying the border, from trucks, horses, and bicycles, to vehicles that can ride on uneven and rough land, such as four-wheelers. Agents in Alaska even ride snowmobiles!

Not Just at the Border

A port of entry is anywhere a visitor from another country will first legally enter the United States. It can be a port along the Atlantic, Pacific, or Gulf coasts; an overland border crossing, such as a roadway along the Canadian or Mexican border; or an international airport.

Even if you live away from the coasts or an international border, there's probably a port of entry near you. That's because any airport that receives international flights counts as a port of entry, as do shipping ports along the nation's rivers. There are over 300 ports of entry in the United States and its overseas territories, such as Guam and Puerto Rico. There's at least one port of entry in every state or territory.

Border Patrol Field Operations Offices

Seattle
Portland
San Francisco
Los Angeles
San Diego
Tuscon
El Paso
Laredo
Houston
New Orleans
Chicago
Detroit
Buffalo
Atlanta
Tampa
Miami
Baltimore
New York
Boston

Nineteen field operations offices oversee the ports of entry. Field operations offices are located in large cities throughout the country and a few smaller cities along the U.S.-Mexico border.

Air and Marine Agents

The Office of Air and Marine (OAM) within Customs and Border Patrol enforces border security in the air and along the U.S. coastline. OAM works with other federal and local agencies such as the U.S. Coast Guard to maintain security on the seas and in the air.

There are two types of CBP agents at OAM: air **interdiction** agents and marine interdiction agents. Air interdiction agents must have a pilot's license, because they operate planes and helicopters to track aircraft that approach or enter U.S. airspace. They often check aircraft that are under suspicion of criminal activity.

Air interdiction agents also search for and track targets that are on the ground, such as criminals and smugglers. They provide **surveillance** and intelligence, or military information, support for ground and sea operations.

Unmanned Aerial Vehicle

Air interdiction agents use planes, helicopters, and unmanned aerial vehicles (UAV) to inspect U.S. borders. UAVs are sometimes called drones.

Marine interdiction agents patrol the Great Lakes and coastlines. They even go out into international waters. Often working with the U.S. Coast Guard, CBP marine interdiction agents follow vessels that may be involved in suspicious activity, such as **human trafficking**, drug smuggling, or terrorist activity. Often, marine interdiction agents work with land or air law enforcement to inspect and catch suspects.

Border Patrol boat

Office of Air and Marine

The Office of Air and Marine also provides special operations support within the United States. Special operations include disaster, or tragedy, response to weather events such as hurricanes and wildfires. OAM was one of many agencies that responded to Hurricane Sandy in 2012. Special operations may also cover special events such as preparations for Super Bowls and visits from foreign dignitaries.

Marine interdiction agents also provide marine response to illegal immigration activities in the ocean and along the coastlines. People try to enter the country in vessels as large as cargo ships and as small as jet skis, so marine interdiction agents use many different kinds of vessels to do their job.

Marine interdiction agents operate many types of vessels, from small boats that patrol wetland areas to larger, high-speed patrol ships that go as fast as 69 miles per hour (111 km/hr).

Cargo Security

CBP examines all cargo that enters the United States. This cargo could be as simple as items driven in a car or as complex as thousands of shipping containers on an international container ship.

Many shipping companies use large cargo containers that link together like building blocks. Sometimes these containers hold weapons or harmful materials. Under the Container Security Initiative (CSI), CBP works together with ports in Africa, Asia, the Middle East, Europe, and Central and South America to screen these containers and gather intelligence about them before they leave foreign ports.

CBP cargo inspectors not only examine cargo when it arrives in the United States, they're also located at 58 ports in foreign countries to examine cargo before it leaves for the United States.

Over 11 million cargo containers enter the United States every year. One container ship can carry containers from hundreds of ports in many different countries.

Agriculture and the Environment

Every year, **invasive species** are brought to the United States illegally. These can be plants or animals brought into the country at ports of entry by travelers or even through international mail. Sometimes, people accidentally bring pests, such as insects or invasive plants, inside wooden packaging materials or even in the dirt on their shoes. These plants and insects can be harmful to our food supply and to plants and animals native to the United States.

CBP employs agricultural specialists to prevent these animals and plants from entering the country. Agricultural specialists are often trained scientists who studied botany (the science of plants) or entomology (the science of insects). They use X-ray machines to search luggage and shipping containers for animals or plants that aren't allowed into the country.

Sometimes agricultural specialists at ports of entry have dog, or canine, partners to help them track plants, animals, and food that shouldn't be brought into the country.

Import Specialists

Anything in your home that was made overseas—from toys to computers to clothes—has to be reviewed by an import specialist. Since the United States trades with many countries around the world, a large amount of merchandise, or goods, is brought into the United States for sale. Import specialists have to estimate the value of the merchandise so tariffs, or import taxes, can be applied to it. They also make sure the companies that made the merchandise didn't make it using illegal methods, such as child labor.

Border Patrol import specialists need a varied background before they start the job. They need to understand business and economics and also have specific knowledge about fields such as clothing, drugs, and other goods.

Import specialists help determine if goods for sale were produced legally. These football jerseys are counterfeit, or illegal imitation, merchandise found in New York around the time of Super Bowl 48.

Canine Teams

Some CBP personnel work alongside four-legged officers. Canine teams employ dogs to help them carry out their work and do things people can't do.

Some canines inspect vehicles, cargo, luggage, or mail for illegal drugs, money, weapons, or even people. Search-and-rescue teams employ canines to help them find missing persons, while tracking teams work with canines to help find criminals and evidence related to crimes. Special-response teams have canines that can capture criminals.

Instructors train dogs in the CBP Canine Training Program. This program operates at two sites—El Paso, Texas, and Front Royal, Virginia. The program also trains personnel at other local, state, and federal agencies. Agriculture detection dogs are trained in a different program in Atlanta, Georgia.

CBP Canine Training Program is the largest canine law enforcement program in the United States. It has over 1,500 canine teams!

Operations and Mission Support

For every program and law enforcement action CBP carries out on the field, there are support personnel who assist field officers in carrying out operations.

Operations and support personnel include purchasing agents who buy much-needed equipment, intelligence experts who analyze data, mechanics who repair vehicles from snowmobiles to surveillance aircraft, and the people who hire all the above.

Aside from support personnel, CBP has offices at 21 U.S. **embassies** across Africa, Asia, Europe, and North and South America. These offices form relationships with their host countries and strengthen international programs, such as the Container Security Initiative. They also operate advisory programs to help host nations and enforce U.S. trade and immigration regulations abroad.

In 2010, U.S. Secretary of Homeland Security Janet Napolitano and a French minister agreed to start the Immigration Advisory Program at Paris's international airport. The program allows CBP to identify high-risk passengers.

Getting a Job with CBP

The qualifications for jobs in the CBP are as different as the jobs themselves. For field operations, agents and officers must be U.S. citizens. Border Patrol and air and marine interdiction agents must pass physical fitness tests.

Many jobs at CBP require a high level of education. CBP employs scientists to evaluate agricultural products, chemicals, or evidence related to crimes. Import specialists must have a background in business or economics, since they must be able to estimate the value of merchandise entering the United States.

CBP likes to hire veterans, or people who have been in the military. Much like the military, on land and sea and in the air, CBP agents and officers keep the United States safe and secure.

Glossary

customs: Taxes or fees paid to the government when goods come into or go out of a country.

embassy: The building where representatives from one country live and work in another country.

human trafficking: Organized criminal activity in which human beings are treated as possessions to be controlled.

immigration: The act of moving to a new country to live.

interdiction: The act of denying or restraining people from entering an area or country.

invasive species: Plants or animals that spread quickly in a new area and harm native plants and animals.

monitor: To watch carefully.

Prohibition: A period of time from 1920 to 1933 in the United States when it was illegal to make or sell alcohol.

smuggle: To import or export goods secretly and illegally.

surveillance: The act of watching someone or something closely.

terrorist: Someone who uses violence for political aims.

vehicle: An object that moves people from one place to another.

visa: A mark of approval made on a passport that allows someone to enter a country.

Index

Websites

Due to the changing nature of Internet links, PowerKids Press has developed an online list of websites related to the subject of this book. This site is updated regularly. Please use this link to access the list: www.powerkidslinks.com/fed/bpa